W9-AEP-783

THE
IMAGINARY
LOVER

THE IMAGINARY LOVER

ALICIA OSTRIKER

UNIVERSITY OF PITTSBURGH PRESS

MIDDLEBURY COLLEGE LIBRARY

A A Z . 5 7 7 2   PS
3565
S84
I5
1986

2/1987
Am Lit

Published by the University of Pittsburgh Press, Pittsburgh, Pa. 15260
Copyright © 1986, Alicia Ostriker
All rights reserved
Feffer and Simons, Inc., London
Manufactured in the United States of America

Library of Congress Cataloging in Publication Data

Ostriker, Alicia.
  The imaginary lover.

  (Pitt poetry series)
  I. Title. II. Series.
PS3565.S84I5 1986   811'.54   86-7005
ISBN 0-8229-3543-0
ISBN 0-8229-5385-4 (pbk.)

The author and publisher wish to express their grateful acknowledgment to the following publications in which some of these poems first appeared: *The American Poetry Review* ("Listen"); *Berkeley Poets Cooperative* ("Beer" and "Years"); *Conditions* ("Everywoman Her Own Theology," "The Unsaid," and "Warning"); *Denver Quarterly* ("An Army of Lovers"); *Feminist Studies* ("In the Twenty-Fifth Year of Marriage It Goes On" and "The War of Men and Women"); *The Iowa Review* ("Three Men Walking, Three Brown Silhouettes"); *Little Magazine* ("Dissolve in Slow Motion" and "Horses"); *The Nation* ("Digging to China," "The Hawk's Shadow," and "Widow in a Stone House"); *The New Yorker* ("Irises"); *Ontario Review* ("Cows," "Lamenting the Inevitable," "Mother in Airport Parking Lot," "Other Stanzas to You, Pythagoras," "Poem Beginning with a Line by Fitzgerald/Hemingway," "Stanzas in October," "Taverna: Athens, 1974," "Terror," "While Driving North," and "Wishes"); *New England Review and Bread Loaf Quarterly* ("Death is Only"); *Prairie Schooner* ("A Question of Time" and "Surviving"); *Tendril* ("The Game"); *Women's Studies* ("I Brood About Some Questions, For Example"). "Staring at the Pacific, and Swimming in It" first appeared in *H.D.: Woman and Poet*; "The Marriage Nocturne" is reprinted by permission of *National Forum: The Phi Kappa Phi Journal,* published by The Honor Society of Phi Kappa Phi.

I am grateful to the Guggenheim Foundation and to the MacDowell Colony for the opportunity to finish this manuscript.

*The publication of this book is supported by grants
from the National Endowment for the Arts
in Washington, D.C., a Federal agency,
and the Pennsylvania Council on the Arts.*

Chasm, schism in consciousness
must be bridged over;
we are each, householder,
each with a treasure.

—H. D., "The Walls Do Not Fall"

CONTENTS

CONTENTS

I

COWS

Dawn breaks
Blue and silver. You struggle against the hangover,
You fight the brutal cold, ice in the ruts.

You have thrown on your black cracked leather jacket
With the Grateful Dead button on the collar,
That you never even think of any more,

To go and breathe the sweet-sour
Gelatinous spoony brew
Emanating around them, filling up

The forty year old barn that was your father's.
Shivering, you curse them, but when all else shrinks,
Money, friends, women,

These unimpulsive bony forms remain
Gigantic as they ever were, echo
After droning echo, shadow after swaying shadow,

Brown and meaty. Like children they lock you
To the land, and all your life
While you lie asleep the flat of your hands

Will rehearse the feel
Of these beasts, or their daughters.
When you lean daily against their heat

And yank-and-pull,
As the milk in its balloons comes down
Pissing into the pail,

You also will sigh and swell,
Halfway between the past and future,
And rub your face, the way you did

When you were twelve and half afraid
Of either milk or sperm
Or blood, but guessed

Ahead to the good, as your father knew you would.

HORSES

—for Jana Harris

What was the first animal
People recognized as beautiful?

Not horses, probably the deer
And bison they hunted and painted

On the dry cave walls
During the long prehistorical afternoons.

But for us it is horses, in herds
And in themselves, vehement and glossy.

Their perspiration, their sleek ripples
Under the hide, their speed.

"Glorious as a horse," you might want to say.
Would you dive into the globular fierce jelly

Of a horse eye?
Solid barn of a body, needle legs—

Taste them in action, how we love horses
Cantering under our crotches, the hard

Facts of a landscape
Changing, blurring—

How we are glad to sail forward, to press
Undulant form with our knees, how we remember

Our parents, their whiskered nostrils, those sharp
Tunnels into eternity, and even

Now when they stop, bent
To our oated hands, muzzles so soft, the horses

Are never tamed, never entirely tamed.

BEER

After the store and the gas station close
There is still the bar,
With its real animal heads on the wall
Alert and thoughtful under their antlers,
Neither refusing nor rebuking you,
Its television they have tucked
Under the ceiling
Like a man holding a pingpong ball under his chin,
Where it yammers like a nervous female
Who uses her hands
More than a person needs to.

Your neighbors will be playing pool, sadly
And easily as they always do,
The teenage women hyped-up, more serious
Than their boyfriends,
The drunkards loud and wide
Like semis cruising down the interstate,
Their bellies stacked, a proud, rounded
Lifetime record of beer to show,
The snaky boys keeping their angular
Mouths shut, chalking their cues.

It could be raining or snowing outside.
Night after night somebody puts
"You Can Take This Job and Shove It"
On the jukebox, and you can hardly help
Loving the familiar bodies, the sounds,
The movements, and how everything goes together
For hours.

WISHES

The dead man's wishes are flying apart like spores
Over his white eyebrows.

Feebly they dart against the hospital walls
Seeking something to attach themselves to,

Shooting for his family,
The nurses, porous fabric, plants, anything.

Forget it. Whatever doesn't get breathed
In by the air conditioner's serious lungs

Will be rapidly disinfected, this is
A modern space, what family, and the nurses

Couldn't care less. The man was eighty, weak,
His larger wishes long ago leached away,

And an ex-President, as they say, a killer. . . .
But if he were eighteen, a fallen soldier,

His wishes would ejaculate forcefully
Into the enemy's air, enrich his ground.

If he were twelve, like the Iranian children
Whose officers send them forth to detonate landmines,

There would be a sudden rushing
Back to the village, to the mama's arms.

If he were Victor Jara's hands in the stadium,
Separated so early, told to

Perform, he would go on playing folktunes,
Lovesongs. Then he would shake himself and start

Playing, touching his crushed guitar,
Liberty's song. Its triumph and lament.

DISSOLVE IN SLOW MOTION

When you watch a marriage
Dissolve, in slow motion,
Like a film, there is a point
Early on when the astute
Observer understands nothing
Can prevent the undesired
End, not shrinks, or friends,
Or how-to-love books,
Or the decency or the will
Of the two protagonists
Who struggle gamely like lab
Mice dropped in a jar
Of something viscous: the
Observer would rather snap
The marriage like a twig,
Speed the suffering up, but
The rules of the lab forbid.
Other rules govern decay
From within; so she just watches.

The little paws claw
Then cease, the furred
Bubbles of lungs stop.
The creatures get rigid.
Has something been measured?
It all gets thrown away.

THE CONTEST

He was unarmed, still the contest was fair,
He was bigger, stronger, hairier,

Could always overcome her,
A hawk dropping on a mouse.

She forgets the cause of the quarrel, the pretext.
It is something he said when they were both awake,

An opinion delivered, a theory
About her book, "Isn't it jibber-jabber,"

Something contemptuous. Get up, she says,
Though they lie asleep, asleep in each other's arms,

Their papers and desks asleep,
Their children asleep, their two cars,

Their matched yellow pajamas discarded,
The angry book thrown on the floor,

Even the magazine crumpled like clouds.
Stand up, she says, and he arises

Perplexed, his thinning hair in disarray.
It is in her hand, swelled bud, a polished metal

Shimmering blue, the size of a jewel,
Or else a frozen and rigid hummingbird.

The first shot wings him in the arm
And then they grapple, her advantage being

He neither confesses nor comprehends his crime.
She gets her right hand free, cupping the gun

She sets instantly to his temple,
Imagines a prayer, and then

The shot enters with a thought's thud.
He falls slowly, slowly, a broken bird.

When he is still, she tosses the pistol
Away, half-carelessly, half-relieved, and climbs

Under the blanket, where it is her own
Brain that the slug is in.

THE WOMAN WHO RAN AWAY

At first no beasts appeared, nothing bright-fanged
And allegorical. I could hear a squirrel chitter
To let me know I irritated him,

So I kept walking, thinking the hell with them
And their letter openers, their crystal speeches,
Uphill above the house, where I could see

The forest floor, past my bluejeans and sneakers,
Many divisions of brown, old needles, acorns,
Quartz hunks, enameled moss. As I looked up,

The distant golden vista made it plain
Everything was more virtuous than I,
The schist more permanent, the shell

Of the sky, like an ingenious artist
Fearlessly plummeting into his heights, more high.
I was the only frightened one,

As if I had walked across Europe
Evading the armies, as if
I had arrived in America like my grandfather,

Jew counting the cost
While the whole country was famous for prodigality,
I, greedy and weak as an infant's fist.

Will I die soon? Why am I alive,
My body leaking heat,
Words of praise misting my lips?

So I turned back and relaxed—after all, I could
Take the car anytime, if they got too dreary,
I could drive back safe to the city.

Only then did the trees begin to hiss,
Boulders to roar,
Mushrooms to writhe from the wet forest floor.

THE GAME

Arrogance and loneliness. If a man
knows only those three words, he runs away
Like a boy, when the larger children are fiercely playing

A violent game he does not understand.
Like a boy with a violin, or a boy
Whose eyelashes are suddenly wet with tears,

And who has heard a rough voice, not his own,
Call "give it back," emptying in a street
Among the grocery and music stores,

The cats, the pavement slates, and the fallen cans,
Glazed, pink, bricky, for it is four o'clock,
A rich smell pouring up from the river.

He digs, he pushes stones with a stubborn tool,
He sets his teeth together, and never,
Never again will they trick and fool him,

Those stinkers, those fuckers, and never
Will he butt his hungry head into the rubbery
Stomach of his grandmother, the wilted and baaing sheep

That rocks and knits, half blind, exactly like
The illustration in *Alice*, and when you touch her
You feel clothing, corsets, and blubber

All at once, embarrassingly.
You feel wet plants, bland food aromas. The boy
Closes his pocketknife and must go home.

They thought he was *her* boy. He is just waiting
For her dissolution into nightmare tatters,
Then swirling animalcula, then nothing,

Like when they blow up enemies in cartoons,
Or you solve a division problem
And it disappears. Like that. Now the boy, the future

Man is running.
He is happy, having begun to understand
The game, the ball, the sticks, the rule.

Soon you will see how the robes float from him,
Clean red and blue, and how the pebbled ball
Drops from the sky, directly into his hands.

RAINY SEASON

The marketplace opens
At six A.M., and it is fair and hot
As a nervy adolescent.
Another scorcher, say the Americans.
The Indian tribes are headed for extinction,
The language loses syllables, the hats
They used to weave are plastic, and their beauty
Is gliding into the cameras of the Americans.

A bare-assed baby chugs a Coca-Cola,
Mud between her toes, her vulva puffy.
A boy rushes between egg-baskets, shrilly
Calling somebody: *Mira, mira.*

Two in the afternoon, indigo clouds
Advance over the mountains.
The enormous drops plummet
Like prayers going downhill. Afterward,
The pavement's slippery with rotten things,
And wetly shines, reflecting heaven.

THREE MEN WALKING,
THREE BROWN SILHOUETTES

They remember the dead who died in the resistance.
It is in sweet tones that they speak of them.
They shake their heads, still, after the dinner,

Walking back to the car, while an evening snow
That has started windlessly, white from pearl-gray,
Falls into streets that are already slushy.

They shake their heads, as we do when there is something
Too strange to believe,
Or as a beast does, stunned by a blow.

"To die in the resistance," they say, "is to fail
To turn into slush, to escape this ugliness.
It is at once to leap, a creamy swan,

Upward." Three voices: oboe, piano, cello.
The high one wishes to be pleasing, the middle
To be practical, the deep to persevere.

A movie theater lobby in front of them
Throws its light on the sidewalk, like a woman
Swiftly emptying a bucket of water:

The flakes are falling in its yellow light.
Then they pass a café, its light red neon,
Then a closed pharmacy.

                        —They pull sharp air
Into their lungs, a pain that is a pleasure.
"Try to live as if there were no God,"
They don't say, but they mean.

A recollection of purity, a clean
Handkerchief each man feels in his own pocket,
Perturbs them, slows their pace down. Now they have seen

A yellow stain on a pile of old snow
Between two parked cars, where a man has peed:
The resistance. The falling flakes, falling

On the men's hats. And now
The snow grows heavier, falls on their stooping shoulders.

WIDOW IN A STONE HOUSE

Dieu a tout fait de rien,
Mais le rien perce.
—Paul Valery

i

Someone was calling me: *Come out! Come out!*
Go from pillows to the ringing cold.

Outside your stone house in October is
The nature of nothingness:

Stars pasted to sky like square green
Bits of confetti, too tiny, too tiny,

And cold excites me, it is hysterical
And greedy, it clangs and ripples like fat

Moon slices sliding across lakewater
In a Magritte painting, it is an owl

Dropped on a chainlink fence, that I am watching,
Freezing, paralyzed.

Frost touches the invisible grass,
The tucked wet oakleaves. I had better crawl

Back through my white door, hearing *Coward, coward!*
As I thrust my icy feet under my blanket.

ii

Don't hate me. In the morning there will be still
The flexible juicy green of Connecticut hills,

High lawns like unfurled tablecloths, glamorous
Windswept foliage furling and rocking,

Cardinals flashing out from gloomy boughs
Across bright patches they will make terribly bright,

Occasional churches,
And everywhere a sense of light and safety.

I'll see all that, outside my window
When I wash my dishes,

My arms pulled forward by forks, knives, tureens,
I pray the fine wineglasses not to break—

It will be beautiful for the weekend people.
They will drive along the roads between the slopes,

Glad to be in the countryside, they will roll
Their car windows down, straining to catch the bigness

Of air itself,
Pointing the beauty out, perceiving it.

Smelling its rooty, complicated freshness,
They will believe there is no nothingness.

iii

Saying goodbye to this world,
Turning away from these loves,

Tasting the light on my tongue—
No, it was not my husband's voice

Or the voices of the mothers.
As I turn over the dirt, the trowel tingles,

And as I hang out laundry, another arm
Sweeps across harpstrings.

Today I feel as if I have eaten fire.
I have never been so alive.

I need not move. I sit and think:
Peeling away this poor husk.

Now the keen cloudy voices say:
Listen. We're trying to find you.
Listen. We think we can see you.

DIGGING TO CHINA

Yes, when the man began to dig to China,
First the sand poured into each declivity.
It was hopeless, he felt desperate.

Then his shovel's rim met rock
And when metal strikes stone, they ring aloud
And reverberate sharply back through a man's whole body

Like a twanged string or the shudders of influenza.
When finally he chopped through the rock
It got softer, hotter, more violent and

More turbulent, the grim minerals melted
Into one another, there was a burbling
Dark redness that hissed and sang,

And the blond man plunged into that center,
Where he fell asleep, as if on quilts, amid the hissing.
He slept one hundred years, one thousand.

He woke up naturally, nobody
Woke him, and yawning, he climbed
To earth's surface, where just

As he pulled himself from the sandy hole,
The sun was setting, the moon with Venus rising,
The lower sky's paleness suffused with juice,

As if from cut plums, nectarines
And cherries on white chinaware. When he raised his nose
To smell, ah yes, it was the early summer,

Yes, there were crickets in the damp grass,
Yes, there was peacefulness on earth,
It all had been arranged.

MOTHER IN AIRPORT PARKING LOT

This motherhood business fades, is almost over.
I begin to reckon its half-life.
I count its tears, its expended tissues,

And I remember everything, I remember
I swallowed the egg whole, the oval
Smooth and delicately trembling, a firm virgin

Sucked into my oral chamber
Surrendered to my mouth, my mouth to it.
I recall how the interior gold burst forth

Under pressure, secret, secret,
A pleasure softer, crazier than orgasm.
Liquid yolk spurted on my chin,

Keats's grape, and I too a trophy,
I too a being in a trance,
The possession of a goddess.

Multiply the egg by a thousand, a billion.
Make the egg a continuous egg through time,
The specific time between the wailing birth cry

And the child's hand wave
Accompanied by thrown kiss at the airport.
Outside those brackets, outside my eggshell, and running

Through the parking lot in these very balmy
October breezes—what? And who am I?
The world is flat and happy,

I am in love with asphalt
So hot you could fry an egg on it,
I am in love with acres of automobiles,

None of them having any messy feelings.
Here comes a big bird low overhead,
A tremendous steel belly hurtles over me,

Is gone, pure sex, and I love it.
I am one small woman in a great space,
Temporarily free and clear.

I am by myself, climbing into my car.

UPPER BROADWAY SUNDAY

It is high noon over upper Broadway—
Depthless and shadowless as a pink Gauguin beach
Over which a green horse trots—
Veronese green.
The trash burns with a stored, painterly glamour
As if it were Gauguin's logs and orchids.
The gasoline reek is majestic
As if it were herring fumes.

Two blocks away, the lordly and slimy Hudson
Sweeps by, a belt of repose.

The shopowners have laughably barred their storefronts
With corrugated steel, to illustrate
Their detestation of criminals, and the sweet
Power, perhaps solar,
That brings murder out in the murderer, love in the lover,
Art in the artist. Haha, that green horse gallops.
He imagines Apollo has swallowed Dionysos,
Dionysos has swallowed Apollo.

II

MEETING THE DEAD

If we've loved them, it's what we want, and sometimes
Wanting works. With my father it happened driving
From Santa Monica to Pasadena
A night of a full moon, the freeway wide
Open, the palm trees black. I was recalling
How for two years after that shy man's death
I thought only of death, how in April weather
I used to lock the Volkswagen windows so nothing
Pleasant or fragrant would reach me, how one time
I saw him staring in a ladies' room
Mirror, and stood in my tracks, paralyzed,
He looked so bitter, until his face dissolved
Back into my face. . . . My radio was playing
The usual late night jazz. No other cars
Drove with me on the freeway. I hated it
That we would never meet in mutual old
Age to drink a beer—it was all he ever
Drank—and declare our love, the way I'd planned
All through high school, picturing us in
A sunny doorway facing a back garden;
Something out of a book. I hated it
That I was pushing forty and could still
Curl like a snail, a fetus, weeping for him.
While I was feeling that, the next things happened
All at once, like iron slugs
Being pulled into a magnet.
This has been *mourning*, I thought; then a sound came,
Like a door clicking closed, and I understood
Right off that I was finished, that I would
Never feel any more grief for him—
And at the same time, he was present; had been,

I now saw, all along, for these twelve years,
Waiting for me to finish my mourning.
At that I had to laugh, and he swiftly slipped
From outside the Buick, where he had been floating.
I was still doing about sixty.
He was just in me. His round eyesockets
Were inside mine, his shoulderblades aligned
With my own, his right foot and right palm
Lay with mine on the gas pedal and steering wheel—
A treat for him who'd never learned to drive.
The San Gabriel foothills were approaching
Like parents, saying here's a friend for life,
And then they blocked the moon, and I was back
On suburb streets, I was quietly passing
The orderly gardens and homes of the living.

Los Angeles 1977/Princeton 1985

SEX DREAM

I see the bare feet on the warm boardwalk
Are my long-haired daughter's.
I dare not look above them, and I do not speak,

Thinking of silvered wood, white sand, cold surf.
The lacquered toenails curl, sand streaks
The downy legs, her cotton hemline droops.

And now the antique carousel revolves
Wildly to ghostly waltzes,
Its riders, men and women, surging and hawing.

About to leap onto it, she has flexed
Herself for that fatality: soon she will seize
A bar, she will climb onto a painted horse,

She who is unable to perceive,
Though she glances to the left and right, the mother
Who stands behind her whispering *jump, jump,*

Or the mother on the carousel, among
The multitude turning, laughing and shrieking, a woman
Who will bow, rise, and salute her

When she makes her move.

LISTEN

Having lost you, I attract substitutes.
The student poets visit, think me wise,
Think me generous, confide in me.
Earnestly they sit in my office
Showing me their stigmata
Under the Judy Chicago poster
Of her half-opened writhing-petalled
Clitoris that appears to wheel
Slowly clockwise when you gaze at it,
And I sympathize. Then they try on their ambitions
Like stiff new hiking boots, and I laugh
And approve, telling them where to climb.
They bring me tiny plastic bags
Of healthy seeds and nuts, they bring me wine,
We huddle by the electric heater
When it is snowing,
We watch the sparrows dash
And when they leave we hug.

Oh silly mother, I can hear you mock.
Listen, loveliest, I am not unaware
This is as it must be.
Do daughters mock their mothers? Is Paris
A city? Do your pouring hormones
Cause you to do the slam
And other Dionysiac dances,
And did not even Sappho tear her hair
And act undignified, when the maiden
She wanted, the girl with the soft lips,
The one who could dance,
Deserted her?

Do I suffer? Of course I do,
I am supposed to, but listen, loveliest.
I want to be a shrub, you a tree.
I hum inaudibly and want you
To sing arias. I want to lie down
At the foot of your mountain
And rub the two dimes in my pocket
Together, while you dispense treasure
To the needy. I want the gods
Who have eluded me
All my life, or whom I have eluded,
To invite you regularly
To their lunches and jazz recitals.
Moreover I wish to stand on the dock
All by myself waving a handkerchief,
And you to be the flagship
Sailing from the midnight harbor,
A blue moon leading you outward,
So huge, so public, so disappearing—

I beg and beg, loveliest, I can't
Seem to help myself,
While you quiver and pull
Back, and try to hide, try to be
Invisible, like a sensitive
Irritated sea animal
Caught in a tide pool, caught
Under my hand, can I
Cut off my hand for you,
Cut off my life.

A QUESTION OF TIME

I ask a friend. She informs me it is ten years
From when her mother wrote
"I hope at least you are sorry
For causing your father's heart attack,"
To now, when they are speaking
Weekly on the phone
And almost, even, waxing confidential.
I check my watch. Ten years is rather much,
But I am not a Texas Fundamentalist,
And you are not a red-headed Lesbian,
So it should take us shorter, and I should get
Time off for good behavior
If I behave well, which
I do not plan to do.
No, on the contrary, I plan to play
All my cards wrong,
To pelt you with letters, gifts, advice,
Descriptions of my feelings.
I plan to ask friendly maternal questions.
I plan to beam a steady
Stream of anxiety
Rays which would stun a mule,
Derail a train,
Take out a satellite,
At you in California, where you hack
Coldly away at this iron umbilicus,
Having sensibly put three thousand miles between us.

I remember you told me once, when we were still
In love, the summer before you left
For the hills of San Francisco,
The music of youth,
To stop fearing estrangement:
"Mom, you're not crazy like Grandma."
It was the country. We were on the balcony
Overlooking the pond, where your wiry boyfriend
And the rest of the family swam and drank, unconscious.
False but endearing, dear. I *am* my mother.
I am your mother. Are you keeping up
Your drawing, your reading?
Have you written poems?
Are you saving money? Don't
Do acid, it fries the brain,
Don't do cocaine, don't
Get pregnant, or have you already,
Don't slip away from me,
You said you wouldn't,
Remember that. I remember it was hot,
How lightly we were dressed,
And barefoot, at that time,
And how you let me rest
A half a minute in your suntanned arms.

THE UNSAID, OR WHAT SHE THINKS WHEN SHE GETS MY LETTER

"Bug off, mom.
You know I love you
But bug off."
Or she passes it to the boyfriend
While taking a regal drag of her joint,
And speaks through the smoke:
"Here's another one.
Jesus Christ, is she confused."
Maybe she feels sad for my sadness
And thinks "Poor puppy dog,"
Just as I at times
Charitably think about my mother.
Maybe she only wonders
How to outwit me.

The honest truth is, it is several years
Since I even pretended
To know what she thinks.
While the pond of our love lies undiminished
Somewhere, doubtless, in the murky landscape,
I am an old bat batting around
Barely missing the trees.
I think how she could yawn, she could tear it up,
She could forget to open it.

THE HURT EYE

It is one week after your accident.
Your friend smashed a squash racquet into your eye.
Today at the famous hospital
The doctors tell you there is a severe scar.
You cannot properly see with this eye.
You may never do so again.
It is what you feared.
You call on the telephone, from the train station, but
You do not wish me to meet you.
My single need
To embrace you is also what you fear.

In this way we begin to rehearse our deaths.
Every portion of our useful bodies
Will forsake us,
Like jewelry stolen from an unguarded house,
Though we lock and bolt, though we hide and protect.

By now you are back in town
Shopping for bread and coffee, being normal.
Perhaps you have telephoned another friend.
No, nothing in life is ever normal.
Later I will meet you at your office,
My buttons done correctly, my lips
Locked, not hysterical,
Showing respect for you, my love, my stranger.

There in your office, the papers are strewn about.
They wait for you, their scientist.
You are one man, devoted to natural truth,
To the inhuman laws that form the wheeling
Galaxies, and disperse them,

Filament after filament, fused
Atom by atom,
Aeon by aeon.

Someone must do it, this work of knowledge.
For a while, with or without your left eye,
You will continue.
As flesh that flies from stars reverts to dust,
Spirit remains, they say, whatever it was,
Not subject to our accidents.
I mean they used to say so.
I am a student of this, an ignorant student,
My love, my half-life.

WANTING ALL

More! More! is the cry of a mistaken soul,
less than All cannot satisfy Man.
—William Blake

Husband, it's fine the way your mind performs
Like a circus, sharp
As a sword somebody has
To swallow, rough as a bear,
Complicated as a family of jugglers,
Brave as a sequined trapeze
Artist, the only boy I ever met
Who could beat me in argument
Was why I married you, isn't it,
And you have beaten me, I've beaten you,
We are old polished hands.

Or was it your body, I forget, maybe
I foresaw the thousands on thousands
Of times we have made love
Together, mostly meat
And potatoes love, but sometimes
Higher than wine,
Better than medicine.
How lately you bite, you baby,
How angels record and number
Each gesture, and sketch
Our spinal columns like professionals.

Husband, it's fine how we cook
Dinners together while drinking,
How we get drunk, how
We gossip, work at our desks, dig in the garden,
Go to the movies, tell
The children to clear the bloody table,
How we fit like puzzle pieces.

37

The mind and body satisfy
Like windows and furniture in a house.
The windows are large, the furniture solid.
What more do I want then, why
Do I prowl the basement, why
Do I reach for your inside
Self as you shut it
Like a trunkful of treasures? *Wait,*
I cry, as the lid slams on my fingers.

IN THE TWENTY-FIFTH YEAR
OF MARRIAGE, IT GOES ON

i

Damn it, honey, neither one of us
Is the victim of the other one, how
About admitting that for starters?

I am thinking about taking
My Jewish mama tragedy mask and your clever
White man scientist mask and—say what what?

Why is this woman laughing
Her horse teeth sticking out
After you've behaved your worst
Possible bullying self, and she
With reason muttered "Why don't
You kill yourself," and you
Ripped through our old friend's screen
Where you sat on his kitchen sill
Three stories up
Threw yourself out his window?

Pleasant September evening
Seasonally warm
A roof
Under it, but I didn't
Know that, did you? Melodramatic, I always
Wanted to live the artist's
Melodramatic life, next time
I'll do the startling thing
I'll have the knife in my teeth
I'll be the star
You can be the horrified one.

ii

Damn it, honey, you say
You wish you'd died rather
Than that I'd been raped
And it makes me grind my teeth.
The fact is, I was raped, and stayed
Alive by my wits, in spite of the guy's
Six-inch knife, nor for
A moment do I think
Rape is a fate
Worse than death, what an absurd
Notion, nor were you
Even home, at the time, to "protect"
Me—can it be that not "protecting"
Me is what's bugged you for
What is it, ten years?
What is this love of death among you men?
Why not wish *I* died? Why
Should anybody at all die? Fact:
You weren't there, it wasn't your fault,
I stayed alive, I saved myself
From death then, from self-loathing later
That wanted to suck me into its toilet
Wanted to clothe me in slime if I'd let it.

iii

Honey, I am not your thing, your property.
You are not my gallant knight, you are
Supposed to be my friend.
But you insult me
You insult life
So I argue, so I drunkenly rant, so you composedly
Explain it is your own
Life you don't care about, which is
Still insulting, so
I say "Why don't you kill yourself
Then," and you do
Your angry performance—I've crossed you!
So what else is new?

iv

Very quiet for a day, two days.
Yom Kippur, of all days,
During which we repent
Not at all, but want to plant
Repentance in the other.
Both of us angry, and
Under the anger, sorrow,
Fear.

Possibly we touched
The silted bottom.
I find I grow sleepy, a bear, a snake.
I anticipate winter.

v

Recovery. It isn't buried, but
Whom would I wrestle with if not with you.
Don't throw me out any
More windows, you say. Check
Out that Kundalini
Energy I reply, and
We seem to be joking and
Making love, we seem
Peculiarly mirthful together, as if
We had a tiny secret, like children
Or we'd died and been reborn
—Which is the sort of junky talk I do not
Ever believe—as if
It doesn't matter how mad
We are, how mad at each other
As if we are in this marriage for life,
Life that is always surprising us,
As my father used to say,
With some kind of kick in the tail.

YEARS

—for J. P. O.

I have wished you dead and myself dead,
How could it be otherwise.
I have broken into you like a burglar
And you've set your dogs on me.
You have been a hurricane to me
And a pile of broken sticks
A child could kick.
I have climbed you like a monument, gasping,
For the exercise and the view,
And leaned over the railing at the top—
Strong and warm, that summer wind.

SURVIVING

Soon the time will come when I don't
have to be ashamed and keep quiet
but feel with pride that I am a painter.
                    —Paula Modersöhn-Becker
                    to her mother, July 1902

We meant while we were together to create
A larger permanence, as lovers do,
Of perfecting selves: I would imitate
By my perfections, yours; I would love you
As you me, each to the other a gate.
                    —Marie Ponsot, "Late"

i

It is true that in this century
To survive is to be ashamed.
We want to lie down in the unmarked grave,
We want to feel the policeman's club that cracks
A person's head like a honey-melon, and lets
Human life spill like seeds, we want to go up
In milky smoke like a promise.
If we're women it's worse, the lost ones
Leach our strength even when we are dancing,
Crying *no right* under our shoes,
When we are working, there is that nameless weariness:
Lie down, lie down, a mule in a dusty ditch
The cart shattered into boards—
Who can urge us to pull ourselves onward?
How can the broken mothers teach us?

It is true that when I encounter another
Story of a woman artist, a woman thinker
Who died in childbirth, I want to topple over
Sobbing, tearing my clothing.

ii

A painting of a peasant woman's hands
As strong as planks, influenced by Cezanne
Who had struck her "like a thunderstorm, a great event,"
That first visit from Germany to Paris.
She was a raw girl, then,
But the thought was clear.
A coarse canvas of an orange, a lemon,
Local deep-red tomatoes, two Fauve asters,
Globes and rays,
Designed like a reclining cross.
A naked woman and baby painted curled
On a mat, lacking a blanket, a portrait
Of what all skin remembers
And forgets.

I walked from painting to painting, I watched this woman's
Earth pigments growing thicker, more free,
More experimental,
Force augmented, it seemed, every year.
"The strength with which a subject
Is grasped, that's the beauty of art"
She wrote in her diary.
And she had resisted the marriage to Otto,
Had wished to remain in Paris
Painting like a Parisian, a modernist
But he had begged.
When they returned home, she knew herself
Already pregnant, delighted with pregnancy.

iii

(1876–1907)
The little cards on the gallery wall
Explained the story.
Language is a form of malice.
Language declares: *Here is a dead thing.*
I cover it over with my thin blanket.
And here is another dead thing.
Please to notice, you soon can feel
Nothing. Not true. Although I did not
Fall, I could feel the heart
Attack, as she rose from childbed, the beleaguered
Grief, in my chest and womb,
That throttled cry, nature is not our enemy,
Or the enemy is also the ally,
The father, the mother,
The powerful helpless hills
Where the pigment comes from.

iv

Only the paintings were not elegiac.
The paintings, survivors
Without malice—can it be?
Squeezed into me like a crowd
Into an elevator
At nine A.M. Pressing against each other,
Carrying their briefcases in one hand,
Pushing my buttons with the other,
Go ahead up, they said,
You have no choice.

Carry us to our floors, our destinations,
Smoothly if you will, do not break down.
On the first floor
When the doors slid open
A child rested her chin on a city stoop
Among the giants.
There were many such scenes, viewed briefly.
At the forty-sixth floor, before
The doors could close, my mother
Rushed inside, carrying her shopping bags
And wearing her scuffed loafers.
Alone in the elevator
At the mercy of the elevator
So much space around her,
Four planes of polished aluminum,
Such indirect lighting,
Such clean and grinning chrome.
An entire blankness
And she was trusting it
To bear her down,
And she was talking, talking.

iv

Today I got a big bargain
In chickens, she says, and a pretty big bargain
In skim milk. Skim milk's bluish
Like mother's milk. Did I ever tell you
I fought the doctors and nurses
The very day you were born. They said

"You'll stick a bottle in her mouth"
But I nursed you, I showed
Them. And did I tell you
When I was hungry because your father
Didn't have a job, I used to feed you
That expensive beef puree, spoonful by spoonful
Until you would throw up,
And then I would feed you a certain amount
More to make sure you were full
Although I was starving.
Did I tell you that one.

Mother, a hundred times.

Did I tell you I was president
Of the literary society
When your father met me.
Did I say that he called me "Beatrice of the beautiful eyes."
Did I tell you about the prize
I won for my poems.
Yes.

The checkout girl at the Shoprite
Tried to cheat me
Today but I caught her.
I told George but he was watching television.
He never pays attention, he pretends
He's deaf. Would you phone me
Saturday.

vi

So my mother should have been a writer. Her mother,
A Russian beauty, should have been a singer.
"She lost the bloom of her youth in the factories,"
My mother says, a formula sentence she is obviously
Repeating, and her eyes fill up like paper cups.
It is seventy years later. Explain these tears.

No promise of help or safety, every promise of cruelty,
Impoverishment, that is our world. John Keats loved it,
Coughing bright red. Hart Crane, also, sank into it,
Like a penny the pig-white passenger throws
Into the water to watch the boys who will
Dive. Explain *St. Agnes' Eve*. Explain *The Bridge*.

Explain these tears.

vii

We are running and skipping the blocks
To the Thomas Jefferson swimming pool
Where we'll both get in free
For the morning session,
You pretending to be my under-twelve
Elf-faced sister, and when we've gone through
The echoing cavernous girls' locker rooms
Where underfed blonds shiver
Knock-kneed as skeletons, the water drops
Standing out on their skin like blisters,
And we're in the water

Green and chlorinous
Cool in the August day
You hug me, mother, and we play
Diving under each other's legs
Until children collect around you like minnows
And you lead us in ring-a-rosy,
You get even the smallest ones to duck
Heads underwater, bubbling and giggling
Don't be afraid! Breathe out like this! Then we all sing
Songs against Hitler and the Japs.
I get to be closest. You're mine, I'm good.
We climb out, dripping on the tiles—
That bright day's faded. Today you are still running
As if you pushed a baby carriage
From a burning neighborhood.

viii

What woman doesn't die in childbirth
What child doesn't murder the mother
The stories are maps to nowhere

ix

A late self-portrait: it's a screen of foliage green
Enough to be purple, and here in front of it
The woman artist, crude, nude to the waist,
Fingers her amber beads, secretly
Smiling, like no man's wife

X

Mother my poet, tiny harmless lady
Sad white-headed one
With your squirrel eyes
Your pleading love-me eyes
I have always loved you
Always dreaded you
And now you are nearly a doll
A little wind-up toy
That marches in a crooked circle
Emitting vibrations and clicks.
Mother, if what is lost
Is lost, there remains the duty
Proper to the survivor.
I ask the noble dead to strengthen me.
Mother, chatterer, I ask you also,
You who poured Tennyson
And Browning into my child ear, and you
Who threw a boxful of papers, your novel,
Down the incinerator
When you moved, when your new husband
Said to take only
What was necessary, and you took
Stacks of magazines, jars
Of buttons, trunks of raggy
Clothing, but not your writing.
Were you ashamed? Don't
Run away, tell me my duty,
I will try not to be deaf—
Tell me it is not merely the duty of grief.

Los Angeles, 1977 / Princeton, 1985

51

THE MARRIAGE NOCTURNE

Stopped at a corner, near midnight, I watch
A young man and young woman quarreling
Under the streetlamp. What I can see is gestures.
He leans forward, he scowls, raises his hand.
She has been taking it, but now she stands
Up to him, throwing her chin and chest out.
The stoplight purples their two leather jackets.
Both of them now are shouting, theatrical,
Shut up, bitch, or, Go to hell, loser,
And between them, in a stroller,
Sits their pale bundled baby, a piece of candy.

Earlier this evening I was listening
To the poet Amichai, whose language seemed
To grow like Jonah's gourd in a dry place,
From pure humility, or perhaps from yearning
For another world, land, city
Of Jerusalem, while embracing this one,
As a man dreams of the never-obtainable mistress,
Flowery, perfumed, girlish
(But hasn't she somehow been promised to him?)
And meanwhile has and holds the stony wife
Whom the Lord gives him for a reproach.

I can imagine, when such a husband touches
Such a wife, hating it, in tears,
And helpless lust, and the survivor's shame,
That her eyes gaze back at him like walls
Where you still can see the marks of the shelling.

We make beauty of bitterness. Woman and man,
Arab and Jew, we have arrived at that
Dubious skill. Still, when one of these children,
Having moved like a dancer, smashes the other
One in the face, and the baby swivels its periscope
Neck to look, I will not see it:
The light changes. Fifteen miles down the road,
That will be lined by luminous spring trees,
My husband reads in bed, sleepy and naked;
I am not crying, I step on the gas, I am driving
Home to my marriage, my safety, through this wounded
World that we cannot heal, that is our bride.

III

POEM BEGINNING WITH A LINE
BY DICKINSON

After great pain, a formal feeling comes.
If that is the case, then after great happiness
Should a feeling come that is somehow informal?

Yes, yes, a thousand times yes,
Like Catullus kissing his girlfriend Lesbia
A thousand times, terrifying the disapproving

Eunuchs, and hugging her too, both of them
Knowing perfectly well what a bitch she is,
What a betrayer, how avaricious, and yet the kisses

Are so sweet, so charming,
As she twists her body alongside him on the couch,
As she opens her lips, like a small animal eating,

So innocent almost, it is excruciating.
Whew, the idea of it, when he leans back
Finally on the satin pillows, and she does also, unglued

And exhausted from all this kissing—
They hook each other's pinky fingers and squeeze, then
Look at each other conspiratorial for

Several seconds and they almost giggle.
But what about myself? Let us say, today for a change
I taught my seminar brilliantly, Night Nine of Blake's *Four Zoas*

Ribboning out of my molars and fingerprints, twenty
New and delicious colors, the students making discoveries
About the Poem, about Imagination, and

Consequently coming closer together—
M. waxing eloquent, D. accepts him instead
Of grimacing at him because he's a wierd longhair

Paranoid schizophrenic and not ashamed
To act peculiar or to talk about trying
To keep himself under control—

Today, as noisy as ever, he describes seeing demons
While meditating, and how he was literally scared
Stiff, nor dared look up, maybe three hours.

Everyone listened to him! D. paid attention!
Scrubbing perception's doors! Furthermore, let us suppose
I have charmed, this very evening, my son from a tantrum

He was wildly flying into after dinner
Like a two-seater Piper into some freak
Thunderstorm bad enough to disrupt communications

With the smalltown airport it is circling and screaming over,
Which I had to do by being so patient,
So balanced, quite unlike myself—usually

If anybody is hysterical I catch it and double it
But this time he touched down, we
Sat together on the couch, eating chocolates, speaking of

Obstacles, like when you think you want to do something
And think you are trying to
But something stops you from the inside,

And he said when bad thoughts came
Into his mind he would slam the door
On them because he was afraid

Once they started getting in, more and more
Would come, worse and worse, and then
You might go really crazy. That was when

I passed him the box of chocolates and said
Not to worry, honey,
That wouldn't happen to him, and we happily kissed.

I BROOD ABOUT SOME CONCEPTS,
FOR EXAMPLE

A concept like "I," which I am told by many
Intellectual experts has no

Signification outside of language.
I don't believe that, do you? Of course not.

If I kick myself, do I not
Hurt my foot, and if I fuck

A friend, or even if I masturbate,
Do I not come? Somebody does,

I think it's me, I like to call her "me,"
And I assume you like to call the one

Who comes (it is sweet, isn't it,
While birth and death are bitter, we figure,

But sexuality, in the middle there, is so
Sweet!) when you come, "me" and "I" also,

No harm in that, in fact considerable
Justice I feel, and don't you also feel?

*Coito ergo
Sum*, you remark. Good, so that settles it

With or without the words. . . .
Meanwhile the errant philosopher

Whatsisname, the eminent Marxist/Lacanian
Linguist, the very lettered one,

Whose very penis leaks
Alphabets, the poor creature, perhaps

Doesn't come at all, doesn't
Like cakes and ale, really

60

Can't taste them, doesn't
Feel pain and pleasure, is afraid to

Touch himself, or admit it—oh, it is
Turning white all around him,

Look at it turning white all around him
Like a special effect in a film,

A kind of confetti blizzard—he won't admit it—
Frowning, tapping, I assume he is a man,

The keys, the dry air
Filling up with signs around him,

Rather frightening, white and whispering, and faintly
Buzzing, the colors draining

Gradually from him
And the rectangles of windowpane—

Oh, this is
Shocking, an X ray flash a sort of

'Twenties black and white, the scholar
A skeleton! The skull grinning

As skulls do! Merely a flash,
But yes, I am convinced there is no

"I" there, I assume I am seeing language,
So that is what he intended, they intended

To disclose. The thing itself. . . .

TAKING THE SHUTTLE WITH FRANZ

A search for metaphors to describe the thick
Pig faces and large torsos of businessmen.
I am encountering a fiendish wall
Of these on the Newark-Boston 9:35 shuttle flight.
My friend Franz Kafka has his nose in a book,
As ever, preparing his lecture notes, while I
Weave among the strangers, spindling and unspindling
My boarding pass, and am aghast with admiration for the cut
Of their suits, the fineness of their shirt
Fabrics, and the deep gloss of their shoe leather.

But what amazes me most is the vast expanse
Of clothing required fully to cover them,
So that one fancies a little mustached tailor
Unrolling hopefully bolt after bolt of excellent
Woolen stuff. How lucky they are, after all,
That stores sell jackets, trousers, etcetera,
In these palatial sizes.
What if they had to clothe their nakedness
With garments made for lesser men?
It would have to be in patches, possibly

Even with stretches of raw flesh showing.
As it is, they look good
Enough to ski on. And they talk
In firm but thoughtful voices, about money.
Only about money. It is not my aural delusion.
It is commodities, it is securities.
"Franz," I whisper, "take a look. What do you think?"
Of course I cannot consider them human, any
More than I would consider the marble columns
Of an Attic temple human. Franz agrees,

But sees them more as resembling something Chinese,
Perhaps the Great Wall. Similarly, they,
Although they speak of money,
Glance from their eye pouches at us, low
Of stature, ineffably shabby (we
Have dressed our best), with "Intellectual"
Scripted messily in ballpoint across our foreheads.
Now as they do so, the athletic heart
Throbs within them, under cashmere and cambric:
"Vermin," they think, imagining stamping us out.

EVERYWOMAN HER OWN THEOLOGY

I am nailing them up to the cathedral door
Like Martin Luther. Actually, no,
I don't want to resemble that *Schmutzkopf*
(See Erik Erikson and N. O. Brown
On the Reformer's anal aberrations,
Not to mention his hatred of Jews and peasants),
So I am thumbtacking these ninety-five
Theses to the bulletin board in my kitchen.

My proposals, or should I say requirements,
Include at least one image of a god,
Virile, beard optional, one of a goddess,
Nubile, breast size approximating mine,
One divine baby, one lion, one lamb,
All nude as figs, all dancing wildly,
All shining. Reproducible
In marble, metal, in fact any material.

Ethically, I am looking for
An absolute endorsement of loving-kindness.
No loopholes except maybe mosquitoes.
Virtue and sin will henceforth be discouraged,
Along with suffering and martyrdom.
There will be no concept of infidels;
Consequently the faithful must entertain
Themselves some other way than killing infidels.

And so forth and so on. I understand
This piece of paper is going to be
Spattered with wine one night at a party
And covered over with newer pieces of paper.
That is how it goes with bulletin boards.
Nevertheless it will be there.
Like an invitation, like a chalk pentangle,
It will emanate certain occult vibrations.

If something sacred wants to swoop from the universe
Through a ceiling, and materialize,
Folding its silver wings,
In a kitchen, and bump its chest against mine,
My paper will tell this being where to find me.

TAVERNA, ATHENS 1974

> . . . το καλὸν
> decreed in the marketplace
> —Ezra Pound

Exactly right
That boy dancing

Who twirls his slim
Girl to bazouki

Music while she
Clacks her high heels.

Four aces and three
Queens on the table,

The shrewd grandfathers quarrel
And puff their cigarettes,

A skewer through
The meat, wine

Pouring and pouring
Smoke filling

The room. It is chaos
Visible, it is no generals,

No brass, no boss.
What joy is like

The joy when the tyrant falls?
Drink, man,

We say to the guest,
It is we who invented the good

God *Dionysos,*
The good word *demos.*

LAMENTING THE INEVITABLE

The world dances with hate
Like heat waves
Coming up off blacktop.

In Jerusalem, city of zeal,
Tante Zillah, intelligent
And compassionate, pours black

Coffee in the checkered shade
Of the oleanders,
Laments that your Arab

Friends finally always
Betray you, they cheat on you,
They presume on your friendship

To put you
In the way
Of danger,

Inviting you where the bombs
Will detonate, the crowd
Will riot. This is of course just

As the Nicaraguan revolutionaries
Invite their American
Sympathizers

To the Honduran
Border where
They are shot at

And barely escape,
And just as the nine year old
Black girl in the Project

Whose haughtiness I admired
When I bravely asked her to play
Looked me up and down

And spit on my shoes. To prove
Something, to share
Something, to throw us safe ones also

Like sticks
Into the fire
Of the burning world.

POEM BEGINNING WITH A LINE
BY FITZGERALD/HEMINGWAY

The very rich are different from us, they
Have more money, fewer scruples. The very

Attractive have more lovers, the very sensitive
Go mad more easily, and the very brave

Distress a coward like myself, so listen
Scott, listen Ernest, and you also can

Listen, Walt Whitman. I understand the large
Language of rhetoricians, but not the large

Hearts of the heroes. I am reading up.
I want someone to tell me what solvent saves

Their cardiac chambers from sediment, what is
The shovel that cuts the sluice

Straight from the obvious mottoes such as *Love
Your neighbor as yourself*, or *I am human, therefore

Nothing human is alien*, to the physical arm
In the immaculate ambassadorial shirtsleeves

—We are in Budapest, '44—that waves
Off the muddy Gestapo in the railroad yard

With an imperious, an impatient flourish,
And is handing Swedish passports to anonymous

Yellow-starred arms reaching from the very boxcars
That are packed and ready to glide with a shrill

Whistle and grate on steel, out of the town,
Like God's biceps and triceps gesturing

Across the void to Adam: Live. In Cracow
A drinking, wenching German businessman

Bribes and cajoles, laughs and negotiates
Over the workers, spends several times a fortune,

Saves a few thousand Jews, including one
He wins at a card game, and sets to work

In his kitchenware factory. A summer twilight
Soaks a plateau in southern France, the mountains

Mildly visible, and beyond them Switzerland,
As the policeman climbs from the khaki bus

To Le Chambon square, where the tall pastor
Refuses to give names of refugees;

Meanwhile young men slip through the plotted streets,
Fan out to the farms—it is '42—

So that the houses empty and the cool woods fill
With Jews and their false papers, so that the morning

Search finds no soul to arrest. It happens
Over and over, but how? The handsome Swede

Was rich, was bored, one might have said. The pastor
Had his habit of hugging and kissing, and was good

At organizing peasants, intellectuals
And bible students. The profiteer intended

To amass wealth. He did, lived steep, and ended
Penniless, though the day the war ended,

The day they heard, over the whistling wireless,
The distant voice of Churchill barking victory

As the Russians advanced, his *Schindlerjuden*
Still in the plant, still safe, as he moved to flee,

Made him a small present. Jerets provided
His mouth's gold bridgework, Licht melted it down,

Engraved the circle of the ring with what
One reads in Talmud: *Who saves a single life,*

It is as if he saved the universe; and Schindler
The German took it, he wears it in his grave;

I am reading up on this. I did not know
Life had undone so many deaths. *Now go*

And do likewise, snaps every repercussion
Of my embarrassed heart, which is like a child

Alone in a classroom full of strangers, thinking
She would like to run away. Let me repeat,

Though I do not forget ovens or guns,
Their names: Raoul Wallenberg, Oskar Schindler,

André Trocmè. Europe was full of others
As empty space is full of burning suns;

Not equally massive or luminous,
Creating heat, nevertheless, and light,

Creating what we may plausibly write
Up as the sky, a that without which nothing;

We cannot guess how many, only that they
Were subject to arrest each bloody day

And managed. Maybe it's like the muse, incalculable,
What you can pray in private for. Or a man

You distantly adore, who may someday love you
In the very cave of loneliness. We are afraid—

Yet as no pregnant woman knows beforehand
If she will go through labor strong, undrugged,

Unscreaming, and no shivering soldier knows
During pre-combat terror who will retreat,

Who stand and fight, so we cannot predict
Who among us will risk the fat that clings

Sweetly to our own bones—
None sweeter, Whitman promises—

Our life, to save doomed lives, and none of us
Can know before the very day arrives.

AN ARMY OF LOVERS

we know each other
by secret symbols,

though, remote, speechless,
we pass each other on the pavement

. . . .

we nameless initiates,
born of one mother
—H. D., "The Walls Do Not Fall"

Half sleeping, for she has been traveling
And should sleep, she takes her pen and writes
" 'An army of lovers cannot fail,' Plato,
The Symposium. No ammunition,
No purple hearts. We can salute each other
By a long gaze. None of us is alone."

She thinks, "I am writing this letter with my blood
And estrogen, true ink,"
And drops the pen. Can a dream appear so real
You think you can chew it like steak?
Hit into it like the leather punching bag
In the downtown gymnasium,
Never getting exhausted?

She brushes her teeth, puts on her nightgown,
Crawls into bed. She is remembering
The man in the three piece suit, the flight from Houston,
His saying "Nuke 'em" to her, flashing
An oilman's smile.

She watched him watch the movie *Jaws*.
She drank her gin and tonic and wondered
What it was really like, being attacked by a shark.
There is a cover of *Hustler* that has burned

73

A portion of her brain forever. A busty girl
Is being fed, from the waist down, into
A hamburger grinder: you are supposed to laugh.
Dear Lord, she is so tired.

She has filled folders and cubbyholes of her desk with evidence,
Photos of flyspecked children, miners gaunt
With emphysema, butchered girls. She thinks
She is like Abraham bargaining with God
On a bare hill outside of Sodom. A thousand
Innocent dead is too many. Five is too many. One is too many.
They shall not hurt nor destroy, a wire twangs in her mind,
Her bargaining position. She falls asleep,
The world aflame and she wants
Not a hair scorched,
She wants everyone to escape.

She falls asleep. And what does she do when the dream
Of an army of lovers becomes her own arm
Burning in every tendon to hold a torch
In the face of that Houston man, to melt it away?
Oh see, her cheeks are wet. Let her friend waken
Warm under their blankets, aware of something wrong.
Let the friend stroke her hair and shoulders, and hug her
Until they both sleep, ink on their writers' fingers.

TERROR

i

If nature is orderly we must create disorder.
If nature is healthy we must create disease,
The snapping jackknife, and in the voluptuousness

Of nature we must invent hysteria,
The sound of a zipper, the flying siren,
The amplified bee in her etherized dance.

He did not say this.—He said
To the pilot and copilot: we are unafraid
To kill, we are not confused like you bourgeois.

ii

The definition of man is defiance,
His wit and will against the creeping insect
That climbs his stalk,

Palpates the leaf, begins to chew, is followed
By a line of others. Defiance,
Denial, disaster, otherwise we are merely

Jerky puppets such as you swine
In your fine airplane.
He touched the .45 to the pilot's neck.

iii

The moment in the toilet when knowledge
Arched up his yellow pee-curve from the bowl,
It seemed, back into his body.

Never, it said, will you be the mother.
You will have no powerful soft breasts,
No jutted nipples, you will smell sour.

The white porcelain forms
Were still there, the mirror over his head,
The cotton shirt rested on his shoulders.

iv

An auto horn bleated outside the window,
Never, and you will never, and his chest
Felt like the time he touched the plug, horrible—

Only the little pee-thing will you have,
It said without voice, without words.
Now, it said, you must forget

This very bad moment,
This very bad feeling.
Go ahead, son. Conquer it.

WARNING

I will no longer lightly walk behind
a one of you who fear me:
Be afraid.
—June Jordan

Let them grow afraid
Not only in the dream
They do not consciously remember.

The dream is: beautiful mother
Slices you up like cooked liver.
Although your shirt is on
She raises you
Writhing upon her fork prongs.
You try to hide
But you are skimming through the air
To look into the lit
Theater of her palate
Ringed like a cave and a cathedral,
Hanging while she casually laughs,
Saliva spraying you.
The dream is: beautiful mother
Takes away her hot breasts
Her sweet stench and large eyes,
Their speaking lashes.
She takes away her fountain,
The dream is your own thirst.

Let them grow afraid
Not only in the dream
They do not consciously remember.

The fact is: Beautiful girl
Wearing a short skirt
And laced boots
Who strides across Washington Square

Taunting you,
Or dumb mud-eyed girl
Behind the Woolworth's counter,
Or fat mama on the fire escape
Sipping her beer,
Bosoms like five pound sugar sacks,
May be a warrior.
You do not know which ones are warriors.
They shall conceal themselves among us.
When you go to rape her
When you fling her open
And think to own her
And punish her,
When the bars of that prison cell sweat,
She may stab you,
Filthy fool,
Your own salt blood may fountain from your throat.

    Let them grow afraid
    Let them grow afraid
    In real life let them grow afraid.

THE WAR OF MEN AND WOMEN

He has come for help,
A talented young man, a poet
Whom I love
But I am not helping.

i

I write in rage against my sex—
What else am I to do? Friend, if your frightened woman
Won't come across, because she's pretty strong, because
She has the whip hand over you, because her mother
And her mother's mother told her: *Use this power,*
Honey, it's all you got, you better make
Them somersault and juggle, make them beg, calculate
Every move or they'll brutalize you, utilize you, take
What you can, sweetheart, give nothing you don't have to—

They did not need to say those things in words,
The ghost grandmothers,
The manipulators,
The same idea rose from the mirror,
The trousseau, the dowry,
The laws of property,
The entrance into the village
Of the army.

Good girls and bad girls, virgins and prostitutes,
Angels in the house and bitches
In the bed, those are our veils, our masks, and behind them
Are fools and smart women, don't forget it,
Crooned the crone arranging the maiden's hair,
The flushed woman slapping her daughter's face

At the first blood, the bones of the dead sister
In the churchyard beside her newborn,
Whining into the ears
Of the sweating survivors.

One might have said, *if you give the milk away*
For free, nobody will buy the cow. Another
Would be praying for her daughter's purity
While ironing. Having broken the chicken's neck,
Another would play with the handle
Of her great kitchen knife—

I write in rage against your sex, although
Here you sit in my kitchen, sipping
My Earl Grey, face perplexed, the sighing victim
Who never reads jock novelists, who never
Leafs through a *Playboy* in the airport bookstore,
Who has not seen *Deep Throat*, the gentle knight
Whose hanging sword is mocked, whose fathers
Burned out their lives like casual cigarettes
That yellow a man's fingers,
In the office, the shop, the assembly lines, the mines,
And never wanted
Anything but a little female comfort.

ii

Contents of one day's mail. Amnesty International
Reports on Chilean tortures, new methods
You don't want to know about.

There is a description of what
They do to dissidents in Soviet
Psychiatric hospitals, you don't want to know about.

My friend writes, the Colorado man
Was convicted of murdering his wife
For what he called deceiving him. She promised

She wouldn't run away after he beat her
Then she did run away, so he found her and shot her
And has been sentenced to two years in prison.

By the way, while you are getting angry
When policemen kill black people
They are acquitted

Or never brought to trial.

I read your mind: you are wondering
What kind of people could
What kind of monsters

Do you know, my innocent friend
As I pour you a cup of tea
Sometimes I want to kill you.

iii

Please, you say
Help me, I can't think
About anything with my marriage
Up in the air like this
Somehow I can't please her
I am just living from day to day
I can't get my work done

Is she seeing somebody
Else, you say, does she
Need a vacation, one drink and she starts
In on me, sneering, we can't afford a bigger
Apartment, she used to want me.

iv

The State of the Union:
In 1973 the "Liberty Oak"
At the battlefield monument

Said to have been a sapling
At the time of the Revolution
Now strung together with cables

But still majestic looking
Master of all it surveyed
Was struck by lightning

Lost one third of its crown
Survives but is
Not beautiful to look at.

v
Forgive me
        You are crying
                I like to see men cry

vi
I run my mind over a handful of names
That lie lightly in the palm as a cone of sand,
William Lloyd Garrison, Frederick Douglas, Ibsen. . . .
The merely clear, the merely rational
Human insight; or Lincoln's *As I would not*
Be a slave, so I would not be a master. . . .
I look at my fingers, stubby, the nails uneven,
Sand runs between my fingers
And the mountainrange names remain, the unchanging
Sculpted faces:
Moses, Plato, Saul of Tarsus, Alp
After lofty Alp, spectacular, and not one
Who desires my life and freedom as his own.

I get tired, don't you,
Of being a miner, crawling around, coughing,
Hacking at dead rock, far from the mountain air,
Of being the boatload
Of refugees raped and throat-slit by pirates,
Of being the drooling infant
In time of famine,
Of being the doctor who explains
Diagnosis is easy, cure impossible.

                    Every mechanical failure,
From your wife's coldness, your limpness, your child's
Stupidities in school, to these matters
Of human sewage touched on in the mail,
My nation feeding death to the wide world,
My vision of the president's pink
Tongue lapping red blood up—
Every one is the failure of the imagination, the failure
To join our life with the dangerous life of the other,
And we would need an archaeology
Of pain to trace the course of this frozen river.

I get tired of this pulpy body.
I get damned tired of telling people
What they already know.

vii

Sometimes you feel on the border: an ounce more effort
Will hurl you into the state of enlightenment.
Your ego will fall apart like the charmed chains
That bound the burning hero until he woke.

You try to recall the rapture of love,
How easy it was to be generous then,
A thread in a vast weft, and the picture
Complete and clear, the millefleurs

And the architecture, the beasts,
The hunters and strolling couples, the zodiac
Framing the edges, yourself believing
Nothing too difficult, and when the ladder

Of soft kisses scaled higher, you leaned like the figure
In the ancient brass astrolabe who pierces
The bowl of our capricious sky and gazes
At last at the true Cosmos.

Everyone who has been in eternity knows
It is not discipline
It is sudden surrender
Merely the fallen walls, the blue, the breeze,
The stairs to the water
And you can nearly smell what you desire

But every minute your pain is worse.

You feel as if you are choking
Or giving birth.
It is like the door in your dream
That you knocked at,
Pressed your face against, kicked,
And finally understood
That it would never open.

                    And I didn't
Ask you to touch me.
Man, stay away,
Eat your cookie, drink your tea.
You falsely think I mean to comfort you.

viii

Heaps of broken stones weathering slowly, a mountain
May break by jointing, cracking, spalling, slabbing.
Sandstone breaks into slabs or plates, schist
Into splintery pieces, cleavages become zones
Of weakness, cracks form among them.
At times severe jointing in massive rocks spontaneously
Occurs when they open tunnels far underground, releasing
Previous pressure on the rocks in those passageways

> So to dig and carry up material
> May release the mass somewhat
> While the worker is the more endangered

Once the cracks are present, water, bacteria and plant roots
Enlarge and wedge the fissures apart. Sedimentary limestone,
The shells of armored animals, goes
Quickly, they say, in temperate climates.

To pass the fingertip over the silver vein
In the feldspar as the rains begin: will the rock crack,
How much of it will fragment this season,
What will the rootlets, the floods,
The swarming nations of bacteria
Accomplish this year, or this century?

Sometimes we wish, O God, the simple blast
That would blow our fossil selves to smithereens,
Cough up the melt, the ash, the inner
Foulness. . . .

It is late in the afternoon.
The white mouse in the laboratory maze
Runs, changes direction, twitches his whiskers,
His intelligence races,
A yellow bar of sunlight, in which gray motes
Are flying, touches his cage.

ix

The worst of it is that we hear the dead
Continually beseeching us
In their reedy voices, droning

Below their other messages, more blind,
More insistent, telling us
To heal ourselves.

Please, they beg, and explain
They depend on us
As all parents depend upon all children.

The dead are in my kitchen
Among the scattered crumbs, the tea-leaves,
The amber tea we have almost finished,

The paper napkins we have twisted and shredded.
They wonder if they can help tidy up.
They glance hopefully from my face to your face.

You can't get there from here, said the Vermont farmer
To the city people who asked directions.

Try it?
Take one step to repair your own damage?

I too want to be healed
By some other person, some wise being, some saint
And there is no saint

There is my crippled self, who wipes the crumbs
Into a garbage bag,
Hands you your jacket back, lets

You go home.

IV

STARING AT THE PACIFIC,
AND SWIMMING IN IT

The mind, she thinks,
She meditates, she thinks

It feels out, it feels out all along
The thinking

Like fingers reaching
Into a glove

Feeling into the
Soft leather fingers

While the other hand pulls, or
Like running down to the warm

Beach, like diving into the
Surf and swimming

With all one's slick energy
Outward, outward

Though the water surges
Inward and outward

According to its own
Mysterious laws, which one

Senses yet disregards,
Feeling occasionally

The brush of some seaweed
Swaying, or a thwack

Of kelp, or a light fish kiss,
Pulling along

The intense red track, constantly moving
Of the sinking sun—what

Pleasure! What danger!
One is then beyond California!

Look around, see how the beach has dwindled,
Lost in

Haze, how the ocean holds.

DEATH IS ONLY

—for Mark and Craig

Death is only
The soul in its rowboat, pulling away.

Wide water,
Wind glances at its hair,

It is taking
Great gulps of the sky.

The oarlocks creak,
The soul stretches and tingles.

It feels happy and irresponsible
The way it did in childhood,

The long summers,
When every day sloped like a meadow

Dotted with dozing
Cows and shady oaktrees,

And the nights augmented themselves
Like a city's lights coming on,

One by one, one by one,
An earthly curtain of lights you could just enjoy

Like a show. Yes,
It loved inhabiting that child's body,

It felt free then,
And it was never afraid.

For years now, sipping
One cup of coffee after another,

Pursing its lips,
It has been frightened.

But why? What did it fear?
It can't remember.

—Embarked, it whispers
To itself. Embarked.

WHAT ELSE

Here is what else the soul does. It tugs me
Like a strong dog pulling on a leash.

It doesn't remember how to heel, or refuses.
Unlike the well-trained dogs in the neighborhood,

It won't obey the master. It puts its head
Deep down between its shoulders, drags me stumbling

Zigzag up the block, while the joggers, plugged
Into their Walkman devices, smirk and stare.

And I have to confess, I am secretly glad of this,
Inwardly sympathetic toward its brute

Will to escape, curious what its world
Of holographic smells is like

To its mysterious doggy senses. And here's
What it causes me to do: sing, dance, kiss men,

Make poems, sometimes fiercely pray, invent
Gods and goddesses though I am an atheist,

Grow strangely sullen at dinner parties,
Forgetful at faculty meetings.

I wish I too could investigate the whole
Garden with my perceptive vibrant nose,

And I wish I too could shed my fur in handfuls
Twice every year; or fall asleep in a moment.

In autumn it elevates itself, it is ten feet high,
A column, a work of architecture.

Springtime it goes completely crazy. Summers,
It likes the beach. In winter, it wants to die.

WHILE DRIVING NORTH

Note: when I drive alone
it is the only time
my mind is entirely free

without obligations
it floats from idea to idea
while driving north

to read its poems
it reinvents the modern

Something escaped when the pentameter
Was broken by the poets. They broke it
Just as a man might shatter a ewer

His missionary great-grandfather
Brought back from Shanghai, purples and tangerines
Glazed over so-beautiful milky whites,

To watch the hunks disperse, or a man might take
A profane axe to a profound piano
Or set on fire his ancestral house

For private reasons, for the energy
Released when noble objects are destroyed—
Should I maybe have said they "busted" it,

Not "broke" it, though Ezra did say "to break . . .
That was the first heave," because "busted"
Captures the quality of small wild boys:

To kill, break, bust, there has to be hilarity
In such an act, think of the matinees,
A skyscraper exploding, a super car crash

Showing the laws of motion, a villain who loses
His footing on a cliff, this sort of thing
Fine as a trout stream full of fishes sparkling,

Or small boys' eyes theatrically sparkling
When they clutch their chests. A colorful umbrella
Of light dispersed by fireworks plunging above us

And the accompanying boom, than which
No sensation is more satisfying.
It is human nature to adore big sounds

That make the chest reverberate, ka-boom,
The steady overwhelming mother's heart
Being the reassuring first of these,

All others then partaking of its safety.
I mean the odd illusion of its safety,
The same illusion when it comes to speed—

I am doing over sixty-five, the road
Is empty, this is effortless, I could
Do eighty-five, I pass cliffs to my right,

A power plant's two chimneys, tan brick, tall,
Handsome, approach me like forgotten uncles,
Drearily sweet old-timers. We meet, we pass,

I think of setting fire to my papers,
The thought lights up, excites me, like traveling
To heaven on a Times Square escalator,

Like love, another flame, a teapot scream
That says: we disassemble in this world
But bubble into an alternative.

Dying people report: you sort of percolate,
And there you are, terrific, your train arriving
At the terminal where many people greet you,

So happy to see you again, you can't believe it,
It's crazy. Up now, up into Pennsylvania's
Lofty humps and bumps, I've reached 380

Where it heads north, the Poconos brown and gray,
The sky meanwhile turning a little pink—
Burning my papers, being free, being happy,

Have I the courage?
When people die they release energy,
Everyone knows, that enters the surroundings.

It's what the person didn't finish using
Or what bound the body,
What buckled its parts together.

This release is called "giving up the ghost,"
And when my father died, for example,
All of us felt a tender spurt of love

He had not finished using, that we might
Use on each other for a brief period,
That could have been poison, but wasn't, it was love,

It comes in through the clothes,
The scalp and skin, no way to notice it
Until after it is inside, working you.

Just the same, when a work of art dies,
Or architecture, if it dies like my dad, suddenly,
Hey, smack, the swing of the wrecker's ball

And its impact, bricks falling, metal springing
Loose and falling, glass dangling and falling,
Oh stay, pleasurable moment—dust, plaster—

So much the greater glee if the wrecked object
Is bigger than a father or a house,
So much the grander energy to capture,

And anyway, they had to kill the meter
Of the old poems, they had to.
Notice how large and innocent they became?

In the true course of nature death makes room
For more experimental life, and the rock
Writing doesn't record tranquillity,

Mostly the land records catastrophe.
Literature the same.

Princeton/Binghamton, 1982

99

IRISES

—for Ross Drago in Berkeley

i

Gigantic purple irises
Were the flower for me that visit.

I noticed their intense
Color, operatic purple, sexual yellow,

As well as their bigness,
Their capacious cuplike design,

Height off the ground
In garden after garden.

I observed
Their power.

They made me somewhat imagine
A hand around them, collapsing and crushing them.

ii

The flower's form is there before the flower,
A phantom form, that the flower

Eagerly dashes up to,
Like a cat climbing a tree, then

Enters and
Fleshes it, fleshes it.

You ask: What could be more powerful
Than the capacity of an organic

Design to die in one instance, and be reborn
Of course transformed, lightly transformed,

In another instance, in a
Thousand other instances.

100

iii

Showing that I meant friendship
I gave you irises

Tall ones
Of the most royal color

Then read your story
Of the gardener

Who told long bawdy
Jokes to his flower bushes

And sang Italian songs to them, so that
They grew enormous.

iv

Being reborn not once
But many times,

Like dots in a child's book, again
And again the picture comes out

And the child paints it. Who cares
If the purple and yellow

Are illusion? Anyway,
They are not illusion, what we believe

We see, we are truly seeing, and it is purple
And tonguelike yellow.

Take these stalks. The blooms pour in our veins
An intense deliquescence.

THE HAWK'S SHADOW

Got to push on. Snowy trail,
Snowfield ahead and around,
The time, what, two in the afternoon,

I'm not wearing a watch and I can't tell,
I'd guess the tree line half an hour below,
Down there where pines drop grit, so drifts

Look like a city windowsill:
This morning I have lifted myself up
Bit by bit over scum

To where the planet's sculpture bursts and is
One lotus burning white in all directions,
Or something set me here. Now it's a question

Of the endocrine system, that is euphoric,
And can believe the universe wants us
To the degree we want ourselves,

Versus the sullen
Muscles, union labor,
Haters of the beautiful.

Weather an unpredictable factor.
Cloudless now, later it may snow,
Filling old cleatmarks, it and I may fall.

Over these switchbacks, the sky, like a genius,
Discovers new depths in itself each minute,
And frightens me, treachery

Dancing in those blue wells,
Able to crystallize and kill
Me very easily.

And can I like being so
Endangered and alone? Oh, mama,
What seems grimace is a pure smile.

Look, things are alive here.
There is a hawk above the icy crest
And there is the hawk's shadow.

Buckskin Pass, Colorado, June 1982

A CLEARING BY A STREAM

What impels the mind to soar forth?
What makes breath start?
What causes people to speak?
Eye and ear—what god is making them live?

> Gabriel, when we were camping, saw a deer—
> > From what does not perish emerges what perishes—

A pale violet butterfly stops near me.
When its wings are closed I cannot see the color.
When it opens its wings and flies my eyes cannot

Follow its speedy fluttering trajectory.
How then can we expect to satisfy
Our hearts with seeing?

Now it's flown off, as I anticipated,
Over the stream a minute, and now has settled
Next to me again, with my sketchbook and pen.

It opens its wings partially.
Staring, I see the pink and blue pigments
Mixing on them, very faintly shimmering,

And the thin brown veins.
Each wing having two petals,
It writhes them,

Independently,
Sensually, unlike
What I expected of a butterfly.

It stands with wings half-open in thought;
Wind pushes them. Its body is solid
Violet, long and hairy, like velveteen.

Again it loops away. Do the weeds and flowers
Take it for another flower, strangely able
To float and alight? Look at that one,

They whisper, it is stemless
And rootless! Is the butterfly to the plant
As the Great Self to ourselves?

It's back. I rest my forefinger
Next to it, and it isn't afraid, it mounts
My ridged finger and walks stiffly across my hand.

Roaring Fork, Aspen, June 1982

STANZAS IN OCTOBER

A long sound when the sky is overcast,
Of honking geese—
Why do we raise our faces, as at a gift?

They ribbon above the mist,
We cannot see them,
These tall brothers and sisters, but memory moves us.

From the known, to surmise
The unknown, that is our habit,
As our pleasure is to recover what is lost.

So, clear and cloudless nights,
When the constellations stand
Over our heads, like embossed paper—

When we prick our ears, like horses
Or dogs, we are listening
For the starry music

Like listening in autumn for the honking.

OTHER STANZAS, TO YOU, PYTHAGORAS

When I said, I would hear the harmony
The stars are said to make,

My next thought was of those
Who would deny me this.

To you, Pythagoras, I am impure,
A menstrual miasma.

And yet I know what you desire.
I desire it as well, wisdom, liberty,

The unswerved will to sail
Into beauty like a harbor, to find

Truth above all. It is hard, the song says,
To like one who does not return it.

I wonder if that is the song
Even the stars are singing,

Sharp and perfect as they appear.

NOSTOS

A pair of tennis shorts in a stuck drawer
Of an old summer house
Upstairs in that bedroom
With the flower-sprig wallpaper.

Every day the surf sweeping in,
A blue-eyed messenger without a message,
With nothing in his hands—
All the same, both before the people
Bought this house, and after they sold it.

So it's alive merely—the house, the laundered shorts—
In their memories, but perhaps it is more
Vital than before,
The rooms more spacious, the hardwood floors
More golden and polished,
The rugs the children kicked and scuffed
More friendly, and the wicker furniture whiter,

The mother's and father's voices more resounding.

LETTING THE DOVES OUT

The imaginary lover, form in the mind
On whom, as on a screen, I project designs,
Images, whose presence makes me dilate

Until I become a flock of puffy doves
Cooing and cooing in a magician's hat, my pigeonblood-
Ruby hearts beating, pure wings set for flight,

For dispersion above the astonished audience
That sits applauding in the auditorium,
Wonderful, while the doves spiral and settle

Back in the brooding hat, tucked muffins,
White contours begging caressing thumbs, the thready
Magenta entrails packed inside each one:

What's his connection with you, oh playful stranger
With whom I have danced drunkenly,
Thinking "The more I dance, the more I want to,"

Eaten the elongated lunch or two,
Talked films, books, carelessly brushed the hand
That carelessly brushed mine, spelling "pretend,

Would you," and for how long can we sustain
These illusions, like magicians' scarves tossed in the air?
How long can even imaginary scarves

Continue to float, to bell out like sails
On a rough lake,
To twirl in the airy theater

Colorfully, painlessly
As the silks in India,
To create a picture of love and liberty?

We ought to leave these matters to our haughty
Daughters, our humorous sons.
Having dreamed so for decades, since the first

Tall gamy lad flashed on that startled "inward
Eye . . . the bliss of solitude,"
I am half ashamed, but only half. The other

Half shameless, no, enchanted, imagines lovers:
Thunders, dry as I am, to invent storms,
To feel their needy pressure squeezing words

Out of my cave as if it were a hat,
My humming, murmuring and dewy cave
Cut in the living rock.

And what of you? You, the reality
Without whom my invention invents nothing?
Oh actual masculine, oh corduroy pants,

Oh imaginary lover, oh father-mother,
I want my liberty, my excitement,
My lullaby, wickedness and goodness,

Like the ensemble of sleepy musicians
Sawing and yawning in the auditorium's pit,
So long familiar they can improvise

A gaudy fanfare while the amused magician
Lets his doves out, murmurs them home again
And draws more iridescent scarves from his sleeve.

PITT POETRY SERIES
Ed Ochester, General Editor

Dannie Abse, *Collected Poems*
Claribel Alegría, *Flowers from the Volcano*
Jon Anderson, *Death and Friends*
Jon Anderson, *In Sepia*
Jon Anderson, *Looking for Jonathan*
Maggie Anderson, *Cold Comfort*
John Balaban, *After Our War*
Michael Benedikt, *The Badminton at Great Barrington; Or, Gustave Mahler
    & the Chattanooga Choo-Choo*
Michael Burkard, *Ruby for Grief*
Kathy Callaway, *Heart of the Garfish*
Siv Cedering, *Letters from the Floating World*
Lorna Dee Cervantes, *Emplumada*
Robert Coles, *A Festering Sweetness: Poems of American People*
Leo Connellan, *First Selected Poems*
Kate Daniels, *The White Wave*
Norman Dubie, *Alehouse Sonnets*
Stuart Dybek, *Brass Knuckles*
Odysseus Elytis, *The Axion Esti*
John Engels, *Blood Mountain*
Brendan Galvin, *The Minutes No One Owns*
Brendan Galvin, *No Time for Good Reasons*
Gary Gildner, *Blue Like the Heavens: New & Selected Poems*
Gary Gildner, *Digging for Indians*
Gary Gildner, *First Practice*
Gary Gildner, *Nails*
Gary Gildner, *The Runner*
Bruce Guernsey, *January Thaw*
Mark Halperin, *Backroads*
Michael S. Harper, *Song: I Want a Witness*
John Hart, *The Climbers*
Gwen Head, *Special Effects*
Gwen Head, *The Ten Thousandth Night*
Barbara Helfgott Hyett, *In Evidence: Poems of the Liberation of Nazi
    Concentration Camps*
Milne Holton and Graham W. Reid, eds., *Reading the Ashes: An Anthology of
    the Poetry of Modern Macedonia*
Milne Holton and Paul Vangelisti, eds., *The New Polish Poetry: A Bilingual
    Collection*
David Huddle, *Paper Boy*
Lawrence Joseph, *Shouting at No One*
Shirley Kaufman, *From One Life to Another*

Shirley Kaufman, *Gold Country*
Etheridge Knight, *The Essential Etheridge Knight*
Ted Kooser, *One World at a Time*
Ted Kooser, *Sure Signs: New and Selected Poems*
Larry Levis, *Winter Stars*
Larry Levis, *Wrecking Crew*
Robert Louthan, *Living in Code*
Tom Lowenstein, tr., *Eskimo Poems from Canada and Greenland*
Archibald MacLeish, *The Great American Fourth of July Parade*
Peter Meinke, *Trying to Surprise God*
Judith Minty, *In the Presence of Mothers*
Carol Muske, *Camouflage*
Carol Muske, *Wyndmere*
Leonard Nathan, *Carrying On: New & Selected Poems*
Leonard Nathan, *Dear Blood*
Leonard Nathan, *Holding Patterns*
Kathleen Norris, *The Middle of the World*
Sharon Olds, *Satan Says*
Alicia Ostriker, *The Imaginary Lover*
Greg Pape, *Black Branches*
Greg Pape, *Border Crossings*
James Reiss, *Express*
Ed Roberson, *Etai-Eken*
William Pitt Root, *Faultdancing*
Liz Rosenberg, *The Fire Music*
Eugene Ruggles, *The Lifeguard in the Snow*
Dennis Scott, *Uncle Time*
Herbert Scott, *Groceries*
Richard Shelton, *Of All the Dirty Words*
Richard Shelton, *Selected Poems, 1969-1981*
Richard Shelton, *You Can't Have Everything*
Arthur Smith, *Elegy on Independence Day*
Gary Soto, *Black Hair*
Gary Soto, *The Elements of San Joaquin*
Gary Soto, *The Tale of Sunlight*
Gary Soto, *Where Sparrows Work Hard*
Tomas Tranströmer, *Windows & Stones: Selected Poems*
Chase Twichell, *Northern Spy*
Chase Twichell, *The Odds*
Constance Urdang, *The Lone Woman and Others*
Constance Urdang, *Only the World*
Ronald Wallace, *Tunes for Bears to Dance To*
Cary Waterman, *The Salamander Migration and Other Poems*
Bruce Weigl, *A Romance*
David P. Young, *The Names of a Hare in English*
Paul Zimmer, *Family Reunion: Selected and New Poems*

0 00 02 0385663 2
MIDDLEBURY COLLEGE